TO: _____

FROM: _____

Play Footsie Under the Table

AND 499 MORE WAYS TO MAKE LOVE LAST

GREGORY E. LANG

CUMBERLAND HOUSE™

AN IMPRINT OF SOURCEBOOKS, INC.

Published by Cumberland House Publishing, an imprint of Sourcebooks, Inc.
P.O. Box 4410, Naperville, Illinois 60567-4410
(630) 961-3900
Fax: (630) 961-2168
www.sourcebooks.com

Printed and bound in the United States of America.

IN 10 9 8 7 6 5 4 3 2 1

To Jill, Meagan, and Linley—my precious angels on Earth

Introduction

Being in love is not a steady emotional state that some of us are fortunate enough to find ourselves in, but rather a dynamic emotional state that requires a continuous series of actions in order to stay alive and well and fulfill the promise of a romantic relationship. It is not enough to believe that the love one feels for another is somehow magically understood. Love must be made clear and obvious. In other words, love simply must be expressed if it is to be known by its recipient, and if it is to flourish in reciprocated abundance between two people.

Most often we express our love through language, as in simply saying, "I love you." Other times we express our love through the written word, as when penning love poems or sweet notes to the one we love. And then there is love expressed in gestures, as in those things we do for one another to give shape to and evidence of the true passions of our hearts. The words I love you, whether spoken or written, are a profound statement. When coupled with an embrace, a walk hand in hand, a stolen kiss, a romantic nuzzle, a game of footsie under the table, or a hundred other tender, giving gestures, these words are elevated to an experience, a lasting memory, a delicate, reflective moment of proof, a love sign that demonstrates you care for me and I care for you in a way that words alone cannot. This book is about showing love signs, those priceless moments we create that cause our loved ones to think to themselves, "I know that I am loved."

I could probably rest assured that my wife, Jill, will love me always and stay with me no matter how little I might do to show her that she is the love of my life. However, because she is the love of my life, I am driven by the desire to reassure her that I love her. I know it makes her happy when I do, and she then loves me even more in return. So every day I do something to show her that I care about her. Sometimes it is a simple gesture, like waking her with a kiss after I have made the coffee the way she likes it. Sometimes it is not so simple, like searching for hours for the perfect gift or writing a poem to hide in her purse for her to find sometime later. These daily gestures aren't necessary to keep her in love with me, because I know that her love is a gift to me, not a reward for my good conduct. However, I also know that if romantic love is left unattended, it will not come to its full potential. Thus, I make such a gesture every day; I show her a love sign whenever I can. I want to make it as obvious as possible to her how much I love her because I want her to love me as much as she can in return.

Jill and I each brought a daughter into our marriage. As they approach their teenage years and become interested in and vulnerable to boys, I worry about how to prepare them for the thrills, trials, and tribulations of romantic relationships without causing them unnecessary alarm. I want them to enjoy dating, but I also want them to be appropriately cautious and selective about whom they give their hearts to. I want them to have deliriously happy, lasting marriages. I want them to never shed a tear over broken promises and dashed hopes. I want them to never know loneliness and despair. When I have these thoughts, I remember how I learned about romantic love watching my parents, my grandparents, my aunts and uncles, and others close to me who had a way of relating that was unmistakable in its meaning—an intense love was shared, enjoyed, and reciprocated. These memories further compel me to be unfailing in my efforts to show Jill that I love her, for I know that I am also teaching our girls a valuable life lesson: what true love looks like. It is an almost daunting responsibility, but also an honorable one that Jill and I fully embrace.

In the end, this book is itself a love sign, another way for me to show Jill that I love her. It is a reminder to me to never take her for granted, to never assume that all is well just because it has been heretofore, to always be attentive to her, to always nurture the love we share so that it comes to full bloom. This book is also a way for me to help our daughters set appropriately high expectations about how they should be treated, and hopefully to tell them what they should look for, in truth what they should wait for, before they give their priceless hearts to someone, and how to then show those fortunate young men that they are loved in return.

I do not profess to be an expert on relationships, but I do make claim to having the gift of artful expression and a desire to help others when and where I can. So rather than give advice, I'll end by simply expressing my hope.

I hope that you will take this book and use it to show someone the love that dwells in your heart, and to do so every day. To that end, a handy gift guide is included at the end of the book. Carry it with you, and when the next special occasion arises, use the guide to select that perfect gift for the one you love. Until then, have fun playing footsie under the table!

Play Footsie Under the Table

AND 499 MORE WAYS TO MAKE LOVE LAST

1. Hold hands at the movies.

2. Lock arms together when taking a stroll. Walk slowly and enjoy a conversation.

3. When the fall colors are at their brightest, rent a convertible and go for a ride. It's a good time for a picnic too.

4. Sing a love song when you are in the shower.

5. Encourage each other to talk about the events in your day.

6. Always sit close enough so that you can touch each other if one of you wants to.

7. There is no such thing as the wrong time to say, "I love you." Say it with conviction—say it often.

8. Let her vent freely about what is on her mind whenever she needs to relieve the pressure.

9. When holding hands, squeeze three times to say "I love you."

10. Share good news with each other first.

11. Avoid withholding bad news. It's best to just get it out and get it over with.

12. Be honest about what you are feeling and be willing to share all of your feelings.

13. Take care not to minimize each other's feelings.

14. Demand nothing from each other, and gratefully accept whatever is given.

15. Expect to receive no more than you are willing to give.

16. Whenever you leave the house, always explain where you are going and when you expect to be back.

17. Be sure to keep your cell phones on when you are apart from each other.

18. Call as soon as you realize you will be later than you expected.

19. Find a reason every day to call and say, "Hey there. I miss you." "I love you" wouldn't hurt either.

20. Never mock or make fun of each other.

21. Try not to be the center of attention. Share the spotlight.

22. Strive to give more to the relationship than anything else in your life.

23. When you are needed, drop what you are doing and give your best effort as long as necessary.

24. When you are setting the thermostat, be considerate of each other. Putting on a heavier or lighter shirt isn't a big deal.

25. Always do more than what you think is your fair share of the household chores.

26. Call to say you are on your way home and ask if you can stop to pick up anything along the way.

27. Be as thoughtful to each other at home as you are in public. Or vice versa.

28. When together in the car, share control of the radio. It will broaden both of your interests.

29. Always call when you said you would, especially when you are traveling.

30. Wait to start eating until both of you have been served.

31. Don't bring the newspaper to the table unless both of you are going to read it.

32. Flirt with each other in public.

33. Learn each other's body language.

34. Lie on the lawn together at midnight and watch the stars overhead.

35. Celebrate the anniversary
of your first date.

36. Never stop writing love
letters to each other. Save
each and every one.

37. Keep a scrapbook of the places the
two of you have been together. Use
it as a memory jogger when you're in
the mood to reminisce.

38. Send a surprise "I miss you" text
message now and then.

39. Read romantic poetry together, especially when times get tough.

40. Write love notes on sticky notes and leave them on the bathroom mirror.

41. Never be late with a birthday card or a gift. You will always be forgiven for a card or gift received early!

42. Only play the games that each of you has a fair chance of winning.

43. Remember to be playful. Having fun together is a great way to strengthen your relationship.

44. Turn off the television some nights and just talk, talk, talk. You'll be surprised how much you enjoy it.

45. Show gratitude for everything she does for you.

46. Understand where both of you are weak and try to be strong there for each other.

47. Be sure to tell each other the things that make you happy in the relationship.

48. Let him know that you notice everything he does for you.

49. Be quick to acknowledge the best in each other and never point out the faults.

50. Compliment each other's appearance. Do it often.

51. Never give a self-improvement book; but if you receive one, read it.

52. It is never too early to say, "I'm sorry." Say it as soon as possible.

53. Learn to be angry at the situation, not at each other.

54. When you are wrong, admit it—and mean it!

55. When you get an emotional response that surprises you, ask why.

56. Before you get angry, let the other person explain. There usually is a reason for everything.

57. If you are feeling defensive, realize that acting on it is probably not the best course of action.

58. Read to each other at bedtime.

59. Let a good-night kiss be the last event of every day.

60. If one of you can't sleep, don't disturb the other.

61. If both of you cannot sleep, sit up and watch your old home movies.

62. Take long walks together on the beach.

63. Go for a ride together on a bicycle built for two.

64. Have a picnic in a rowboat.

65. Share secrets with each other that no one else knows about.

66. Always keep your mate's confidences private—it is a matter of character and fidelity.

67. Always speak to each other with respect. Never shout at each other.

68. Whatever the problems may be, work for harmony, not just peaceful coexistence.

69. Be transparent in the way you live. Never do anything you wouldn't want the other to know about.

70. Make a commitment never to correct each other in front of others or argue in public.

71. Give other couples watching you reason to say, "I wish we were like that."

72. Go on a picnic together on the first warm weekend of spring.

73. Play footsie under the table.

74. Reach across the table and hold hands while toasting each other.

75. Order one decadent dessert to share, and feed it to each other.

76. Bring him lemonade while he is cutting the grass.

77. Keep a calendar of special moments in earlier years, and celebrate those moments each time that date comes around again.

78. Wash the car together.

79. Buy matching coffee cups the next time you go shopping.

80. Help each other fold the laundry.

81. Play each other's favorite music when you go for a ride.

82. When you're on a long trip, take turns driving and sleeping.

83. Go out dancing on a Saturday night. If you can't dance, learn.

84. On a snowy evening, go outside together and catch snowflakes on your tongues.

85. Never pass up a ride through the Tunnel of Love.

86. Decorate the house together for the holidays.

87. When you are walking together in the rain, hold most of the umbrella over her.

88. When you're in a setting where you should be quiet, mouth the words "I love you."

89. Learn how to say "I love you" in sign language.

90. When he is stressed out, massage his head and neck. He'll return the favor.

91. Compromise quickly, never as a last resort.

92. Emphasize the things about each other that make you happy rather than those that might not be as endearing.

93. When the bathroom door is shut, don't try to enter.

94. Just ignore each other's weird noises.

95. Understand that she will use more than half of the closet space and bathroom counter. Just accept it and move on.

96. Sleep late on Saturdays
   when possible.

97. Understand that he will collect
   lots of tools and obsess about the
   grass. Just accept it and move on.

98. When spending the day
   together, leave the watches
   at home.

99. The best-laid plans can be a
   bore. Leave a little room for
   something unexpected.

100. Always cherish the moments you share. You never know how many more you will have.

101. Be willing to go where the other wants to go, even if it's not your preference.

102. Encourage each other to spend as much time with friends as possible.

103. Never complain about each other to your parents.

104. Even though you are a guest, pitch in and help your in-laws with whatever needs doing.

105. Find out what each of you admires about your parents, and strive for that in your own relationship.

106. Allow him the harmless horseplay he enjoys with the guys.

107. Be cordial to the people in each other's lives, and treat them as if they are important to you too.

108. Never complain about visiting each other's parents or other family members.

109. Always agree ahead of time how long a visit will last.

110. Reassure each other whenever one of you needs it, no matter how often.

111. Make the focus of your relationship each other's hearts, not your bodies.

112. Try to be the first to say "I love you" in any situation where it is appropriate.

113. Send each other flowers at the office. Don't send the same flowers every time.

114. Be sure to include a unique romantic message with every gift.

115. Wait on each other hand and foot on your birthdays.

116. Plan ahead and celebrate birthdays in grand fashion.

117. Be considerate, even if you don't understand why she is upset.

118. Never point a finger in anger.

119. Remember that it is important to talk through your differences. Don't "just drop it." It will fester.

120. Be patient, even if you
asked him not to be late.

121. Forgive and forget every offense,
without exception. The more
difficult it is to forgive, the more
important it is to do so.

122. Become adept at forgetting.
Harboring resentment will
erode the best in each of you.

123. Give each other the passwords
to your email.

124. Never open each other's mail.

125. Shop together for furniture and the artwork you use in decorating your home.

126. For a change, go shopping together and each of you pick out something for the other.

127. Never leave each other "to do" lists.

128. Look for the things you can agree upon and focus on them.

129. Fulfill all your responsibilities to each other willingly. Don't be afraid to go the second mile.

130. Don't complain if there is a third or fourth mile.

131. Thank each other for little things as often as you can.

132. Treat each other so well that your confidence in each other never wavers.

133. It is important to trust each other and even more important to be trustworthy.

134. When one of you says no, respect it.

135. Set out with no destination in mind. Enjoy the process of getting somewhere together.

136. Nag each other about staying healthy.

137. Never let your life get so busy that you don't have time for each other.

138. Be each other's best friend.

139. Tell each other stories about the funny things that happened when you were children.

140. Be sure to reciprocate every gesture of patience, affection, kindness, assistance, and unselfishness.

141. Be uninhibited in showing affection—not obnoxious, just enthusiastic.

142. Just for fun, carry her across the threshold occasionally.

143. Remember, everybody enjoys having their back scratched!

144. The same goes for foot massages.

145. Just for fun, wear nothing but a bathrobe now and then.

146. Enjoy big mugs of hot cocoa with marshmallows together on the first day of winter.

147. Stay in good physical shape for each other.

148. Encourage each other in everything you do.

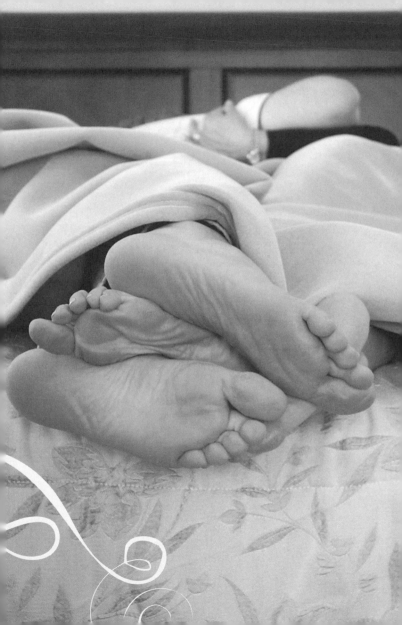

149. If you don't want to know the answer, don't ask the question.

150. Work hard to break your bad habits, and don't go back to them.

151. Always accept help when it is offered.

152. Never demand an apology. Wait for it to arrive in its own time.

153. Keep a jar for loose change. When it is full, cash it in together and use the money to buy something fun and frivolous.

154. Put some creativity and effort into the gifts you select. Never give gift certificates. See the back of this book for ideas you can keep in your wallet.

155. Always personalize the cards you give to each other.

156. Surprise each other with hugs and kisses when they are least expected.

157. Give him the gift he wants, not the one you think he needs.

158. Buy a gift bag, fill it with sixty Hershey's Kisses, and give it with a note that says, "For every minute of the hour that I think about you."

159. Wake each other with gentle hugs and kisses. Keep breath mints on your nightstand for just this occasion.

160. Make a wish for each other at every full moon.

161. Cook a meal together, and eat it by candlelight, listening to the soundtrack of a romantic movie.

162. Take naps together on rainy afternoons. And sunny ones too. And when it snows. And...

163. Try new adventures together at least once a month, and save mementoes of the occasion.

164. Take pictures of every special occasion you share. Look at them together later.

165. Keep a relationship journal and read to each other often from it.

166. Display photographs of the two of you doing fun things together.

167. Be patient when you think you know what needs to be done but he hasn't figured it out yet.

168. Respect each other's everyday responsibilities—demanding constant attention is selfish.

169. Emphasize the positive in your relationship—don't focus on the negative.

170. Be sure to remind each other how blessed you are to have one another.

171. Overlook the messes made if he or she was only trying to help you in the first place.

172. Expect that there will be bad times. Prepare for them by creating so many good times that the bad ones are easily outnumbered.

173. If you get a nice bonus, don't hide it. It belongs to both of you.

174. Spend any leftover money on each other, not yourself. Be generous, not selfish.

175. Let her put her feet in your lap; kiss her toes when she does.

176. Let her wear your shirts, and don't complain if she wants to keep one for herself.

177. Smile whenever you catch each other's eye, regardless of where you are.

178. The next time there is warm summer rain, go outside and slow dance in it.

179. Shave his neck for him; use warm water and a sharp razor.

180. Sneak a kiss in public once in a while, when it is least expected. Be discrete.

181. Share a warm bubble bath after a hard day. Wash each other's backs.

182. Linger in admiration of each other's best attribute.

183. Be sure to keep a photograph of each other in your purse or wallet.

184. Send each other goofy cards for no particular reason.

185. When you're going out to celebrate a special occasion, let the maître d' know about it before you arrive.

186. Watch each other's favorite movies together.

187. If you must comment on the staring actress, let it be only about her acting.

188. Avoid asking him, "Why don't you say things like that?" after the leading actor's most romantic lines.

189. Never quiz each other about anything that may have been said while sleeping.

190. Throw away photos of old girlfriends or boyfriends.

191. Should you one day have children together, devote yourself to them above everything else.

192. Always make lots of time available to your children, and help each other take care of them.

193. Agree upon how to raise the children. Do not criticize each other's actions in front of them.

194. If each of you has children from a previous marriage, help each other to become the best stepparent possible.

195. Make the bed.

196. Talk about a special moment you both have experienced that you wished would never end. Make it happen again.

197. Plan to have at least one date every week, and do some of the things you did when you were first dating.

198. Lead each other to a candlelit bathroom and a hot bath.

199. Celebrate the anniversary of your first date by doing it all over again.

200. Chase each other around the house once in a while. Get caught.

201. Whisper in each other's ears, "I can't wait to get you home" and "You are so hot!" whenever you can.

202. Listen to each other. Really listen. Listen some more.

203. Share all the secrets you can without hurting each other.

204. If either of you is uncomfortable with the plan, change it immediately.

205. Be each other's sounding board, even if you have heard it before.

206. Go to an amusement park and ride the Ferris wheel—kiss when you reach the top.

207. Try to win a prize for her at the fair. Spend whatever it takes.

208. Be each other's biggest fan—and loudest cheerleader.

209. Have a beer with him at the ball park. Stand and holler whenever he does.

210. Attend each other's high school and college reunions.

211. Give each other lucky charms.

212. Never suggest plastic surgery or a diet.

213. Never have a crush on a celebrity. Or at least don't confess to it.

214. Don't ever say or do anything that will cause someone else to think you are available.

215. When you have important decisions to make, ask each other for advice.

216. Never remind each other of how fit and slender you once were.

217. Confide in each other—first and often.

218. Never use offensive words or gestures—or ones that provoke fear.

219. Don't ask for details of any previous relationship.

220. Always act toward each other in ways that you will never regret later.

221. Don't ever make the same mistake twice. Learn from your mistakes.

222. Become skilled in the fine arts of overlooking and overcoming.

223. Go out of your way to start a conversation on something that is important to her.

224. Share your deepest personal and religious beliefs with each other.

225. Pray together when times are tough.

226. Show genuine concern about the things that keep your partner awake at night.

227. If you are religious, attend worship services together and become involved in the congregation's activities as much as you can.

228. Find a charity or non-profit organization you both believe in and serve as volunteers together.

229. When you watch the sunset together, be sure to say, "Thank you for spending this day with me," once it disappears.

230. When you watch the sunrise together, remember to say, "I'm so glad I have another day with you," the moment it appears.

231. Always look into each other's eyes when you are talking.

232. Take care of the routine maintenance of her car, and keep her gas tank full.

233. When you find that you are about to eat or use the last of something, offer to share it. Better yet, give it to your mate.

234. When you shower or bathe, don't use up all the hot water.

235. Do each other's chores once in a while.

236. Clean up after yourself. Don't leave a mess for your partner.

237. Arrange for a lawn service to give your partner a well-deserved break one weekend.

238. They're your friends, not hers. Don't expect her to take care of them for you.

239. When your mate says, "We need to talk," understand that means right now, not later.

240. Don't play one-upmanship with your mate. No one ever wins.

241. If you know it is irritating, stop doing it.

242. They're your friends, not his. Don't expect him to drop everything just because they came over.

243. Never say, "You've changed," unless both of you would agree that it's for the better.

244. When you can see that help is needed, get in there and help before you are asked to do so.

245. Celebrate with each other in times of joy.

246. If you can help each other's dreams come true, do it.

247. Support each other's efforts at personal growth.

248. Encourage each other's individuality.

249. Do not compete with the children for each other's time—but make time for everybody in the family.

250. Alternate holidays between your families. Do it without complaint.

251. Invite both of your families to join together in celebrating special events in your lives.

252. Participate in each other's family traditions as if they have been your own for generations. It will enrich your life.

253. Be enthusiastic about getting to know each other's families.

254. If each of you has children from a previous marriage, treat all of them equally in your estate planning.

255. If your family includes a child that isn't yours, love him or her as if they were.

256. Treat each other like you would want someone to treat your son or daughter.

257. Go to any length to make each other laugh.

258. Play to have fun, not to win. Play often.

259. Love is a team sport, not a competition. You don't have to win to have a good time.

260. When you're together, try to find something humorous in every situation.

261. Be her gentleman. Go outside for the paper. Take out the dog. Take out the trash. Unload the dishwasher.

262. When you're watching TV on the couch together, be the one who refreshes the beverages.

263. Change your routine once in a while to add a little spice to your relationship.

264. Be his siren. Rub his shoulders. Let your hair down. Wear the perfume he bought for you. Sleep naked.

265. Say "Thank you for loving me" often.

266. End every telephone conversation with "I love you."

267. There will always be more work to do. Take time to relax together.

268. Be generous—with your time, your attention, your money. And your love.

269. Stand or walk between her and traffic.

270. Say "Thanks, honey" or wink at him when he holds the door for you.

271. Give heart-shaped candy on the anniversary of your first date.

272. Be willing to stop anything that you are doing to make time for a little romance.

273. Every ten years or so, invite your family and closest friends to a party in which you renew your vows.

274. Wait on each other hand and foot
on your anniversary.

275. Always follow your heart, not
your friends' recommendations.

276. Call each other's parents
on special occasions.

277. On the anniversary of your
first date, share that same
lingering good-night kiss
you both still remember.

278. Answer unambiguously if someone asks if you are in a relationship.

279. After saying yes, pull out your wallet and show off your pictures.

280. Affirm each other's strengths, and never exploit the weaknesses.

281. Never lead in a direction where the other doesn't want to go.

282. Never tell a lie in order to get out of an embarrassing situation.

283. If the two of you run into one of her old boyfriends, be a gentleman.

284. If the two of you run into one of his old girlfriends, forget about her as soon as possible.

285. Never put yourself in a situation that will tempt you to lie if you get caught.

286. When you make a promise, keep it. A good relationship requires keeping your promises.

287. Be sure to share the power and control in your relationship.

288. Allow each other to be an expert in something.

289. If she forgot her gloves or jacket, give her yours.

290. If she forgot her sunglasses,
give her yours.

291. If she forgot her pajamas,
hide yours.

292. If he forgot his toothbrush,
give him yours.

293. If he forgot his razor,
give him yours.

294. If he brought his pajamas,
hide them.

295. Let your touch be gentle,
never demanding or rough.

296. Never, ever tell anyone
each other's secrets.

297. Talk in detail about what it
is that keeps you in love.

298. Talk freely about the fun and
good times you have shared.

299. The next time you go out to eat together, secretly check into a hotel first and surprise your partner with the key at the end of the meal.

300. When you are traveling and you call home, say, "I wish I were there with you."

301. If you must travel alone, always bring a little something back for the other.

302. The next time she mentions she needs to go shopping, go with her, double her budget, and carry all the bags. Don't complain about how long it takes.

303. When you are traveling alone, call home every day—sometimes more than once.

304. When one of you needs a hug, give two.

305. When questions are asked, be honest in your answers, but be tactful and considerate in how you answer.

306. Turn down the television when the other person is on the phone.

307. When he goes out on the town with his friends, don't demand to know everything that happened as soon as he gets home.

308. Be sure not to monopolize the conversation, and don't make your stories too long. After all, you're not the only person who has something to say.

309. Don't sneak around reading each other's text messages.

310. When she goes out with her girlfriends, don't call her every fifteen minutes to find out when she is coming home.

311. Take time to enjoy a glass of wine or a cup of tea together while sitting on the porch.

312. Make a habit of going for an evening stroll during a full moon.

313. Give most of your spare time to each other, and when it seems like there isn't any, make some.

314. Don't wait until Valentine's Day to say, "Thank you for being mine."

315. Don't minimize or make fun of the things she does to make herself feel beautiful.

316. Don't be jealous. Don't be a snoop.

317. Don't play hard-to-get.

318. Remember, neither of you owe the other anything. Your relationship is a gift.

319. Don't laugh out loud at or tell others about what he does when he doesn't know you are watching him.

320. Never be flirtatious with each other's friends.

321. Never compare each other to old flames or ex-spouses.

322. Slow dance together occasionally in the shower.

323. Keep scented massage oil close at hand.

324. Understand the difference between sexy and kinky.

325. Explore each other in the dark.

326. Buy an umbrella for her to keep in her car.

327. Keep your clothes and other things picked up.

328. Don't surprise your mate
by putting your cold feet
where they don't belong.

329. Paint her toenails.

330. Practice breath parity. Either
both of you eat garlic, or both
of you skip it.

331. Give him a grooming kit to
keep at the office.

332. Wash each other's hair.

333. Always make him feel desirable and appreciated—especially if you want him to feel the same way about you.

334. Give her time when she needs it—she will come to you when she is ready.

335. Agree on goals that you can pursue in your life together, and keep looking for new ones to add.

336. Every now and then review your goals together. Celebrate the ones that were met.

337. Remember to share the credit for all that has turned out according to your plan.

338. When your mate is talking to you, don't make "hurry up" hand gestures.

339. Be sure your behavior and attitudes show that you want to be together for the rest of your lives.

340. When you kiss while stopped at a traffic light, remind each other of the first time you did that.

341. When he is trying his best to express himself, smile and hold his hand to comfort and encourage him.

342. Kiss before you leave the house, each and every time.

343. Kiss again as soon as you get home. Times in between are okay too.

344. Never storm off when you are mad; never slam a door.

345. Never break anything in anger. Not only may you not be able to replace it, it's bad form.

346. Be careful about how you talk to one another. The pain of hurtful words can last a long time.

347. Be careful not to do anything that will lessen your respect for each other.

348. It is very important to understand that no matter how well you know each other, there will always be things you don't understand.

349. Ask when you don't understand. Avoid guessing.

350. Remember, everyone needs a little space now and then. Respect it when it is requested.

351. Just for fun, pretend you are strangers and get to know each other again.

352. Surprise each other with a back rub now and then.

353. Always strive to learn something new about each other.

354. In your own way, reciprocate every gesture of affection made toward you.

355. When your partner asks, "What are you thinking about?" say something, almost anything, but never, "Nothing."

356. Always be sure to introduce each other to anyone you meet.

357. If you say you will do something, do it. If you said you won't, don't!

358. Never keep score of the times when you have been hurt or offended.

359. If you aren't in the mood, that's okay, but do something at a later time to encourage your partner's desire for you.

360. Resist the temptation to think yourself a relationship expert just because you saw something on TV.

361. Don't act like you know everything. You don't.

362. Ask for each other's opinions, and show respect by listening to the entire answer before replying.

363. Don't sweat the small stuff. It probably doesn't matter anyway.

364. Take the best of your individual traditions and make them a part of your relationship. Forge new traditions together also.

365. Make an effort to learn about the things that interest your mate. You might be surprised to learn that you find them interesting too.

366. Remember that most of the time compromise is more important than agreeing on who is right.

367. Surprise her by singing her favorite love song to her on your wedding anniversary.

368. Surprise him with a romantic and affectionate evening on your wedding anniversary.

369. Think of reasons why you have never felt the same way about anyone else, and share them.

370. Always include a message with any gift you give.

371. If you are going to buy clothing for each other, then make sure it's the right size.

372. Give her a nickname that makes her feel like a queen.

373. Show off for each other once in a while.

374. Learn how to say "I love you" in a different language.

375. Carve your initials in a tree.

376. Write your names in cement. Encircle them with a heart.

377. Give him a nickname that makes him feel like a stud.

378. Take lots of pictures of each other, and make a photo history of your relationship.

379. Make a time capsule together, and open it on a milestone anniversary.

380. Keep pictures of each other on your nightstand.

381. Have a warm towel ready and waiting when your partner gets out of the shower.

382. Reach into the shower and scrub your partner's back.

383. Use lotion on your rough spots.

384. Serve breakfast in bed once in a while. Try feeding each other.

385. If you are offered a breath mint, say "thank you" and use it.

386. Surprise each other with sexy underwear.

387. Always notice what she does to her hair.

388. Bring home wine, roses, or champagne for no reason at all.

389. Send romantic emails to each other.

390. Know each other's favorite color and favorite foods.

391. Praise him when he loses weight, even if only a couple of pounds.

392. Send romantic cards and letters to each other in the mail.

393. If asked, "Do you still love me?" always answer, "More than ever."

394. Write short but profound messages for each other and leave them where they are sure to be found.

395. Only take the risks that both of you are comfortable with.

396. If you must change the schedule, tell each other beforehand—as soon as you realize it must be changed.

397. Seize every opportunity to tell her she is beautiful.

398. Thank each other for the happy memories of things you've done together.

399. Remember the birthdays of each of your parents.

400. Always pick up the check when dining out with either set of parents.

401. Always thank him for the hard work he does.

402. Celebrate each other's achievements, especially those that required much effort.

403. Always give each other the benefit of the doubt.

404. Praise each other in front of your friends.

405. When you're at a wedding together, dance as if it's all about you.

406. The next time you watch a romantic movie together, try acting out some of your favorite scenes.

407. When your partner says, "You look sexy in that," wear it again, soon.

408. In five minutes or less, make lists of why you love each other and share them together.

409. If she needs your attention, give it.

410. If she picked it out for you, wear it.

411. If she asks you to get rid of it, chuck it.

412. Listen carefully for hints of places she would like to go. Find a way to take her there.

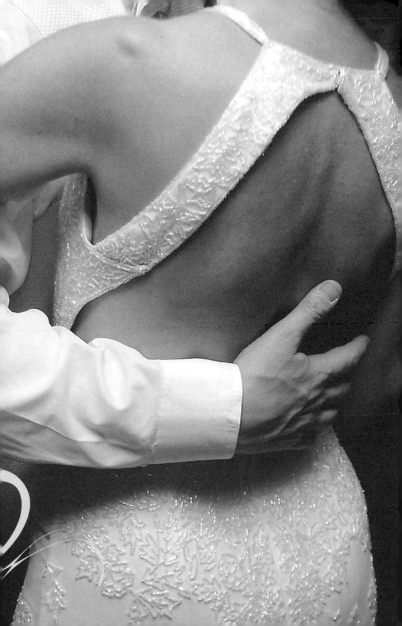

413. If he asks you to go along, go.

414. If he asks for hints, give them.

415. If he gave it to you, use it.

416. Surprise him by making arrangements for a getaway weekend.

417. Try to anticipate each other's needs, and fulfill them in abundance.

418. Remember that sometimes you cannot see things clearly, and in those times, have trust.

419. Make sure your mate never feels lost.

420. Give each other every reason to want to snuggle before falling asleep.

421. Trust—and be trustworthy.

422. When the two of you are in the presence of other women, always keep your eyes on her.

423. Let your "yes" mean yes, and your "no" mean no.

424. Let your "I do" always mean "I won't with anyone else."

425. Never do anything you would not want to have to admit to the other.

426. When the two of you are in the presence of other men, always kiss him at least once for all to see.

427. If you must have a conversation with an old flame, keep it short. Don't keep it a secret.

428. Never blame each other when things don't turn out as well as you wished they had.

429. Let your business with your ex be just that—business.

430. Bring home a surprise gift—
just for the pleasure of seeing
the reaction.

431. Wear your wedding ring every
day. Wear it with pride.

432. Always stand up for each other.

433. Be quick to believe good
things about each other
and slow to believe bad.

434. When she walks past, reach out to
touch her.

435. Remember that you are stronger together than when apart. Spend most of your time together.

436. When you are away, try to get home early if you can.

437. When one of you has been away from home, buy flowers to celebrate their return.

438. When he reaches for you, move closer.

439. Look for reasons to begin a sentence with "I really appreciate it when you…"

440. When one of you is sick, clear your schedule and spend the day taking care of the other.

441. Surprise her by adding a few of your own words to your wedding vows. She will never forget it.

442. Walk up to him and say, "You may now kiss the bride." He'll gladly do it every time.

443. Make a big deal of every anniversary of your relationship milestones.

444. Strive to show your love in as many ways as possible. A few ways are simply too few.

445. Learn how to make your partner's favorite drink.

446. If you want to eat off each other's plate, ask first.

447. On New Year's Eve, celebrate till the wee hours of the morning.

448. Treat each other to a weekend brunch at a favorite restaurant.

449. Keep your mate's favorite snack in the pantry.

450. Listen carefully for hints of things your partner would like to have. Surprise each other by giving them as gifts at unexpected times.

451. Plan a costume party together and invite your friends. Dress alike.

452. When you're at a party, pay more attention to each other than to anyone else.

453. Always acknowledge it when your partner tells you, "I love you."

454. Understand that he may not always use the most obvious words to tell you he loves you.

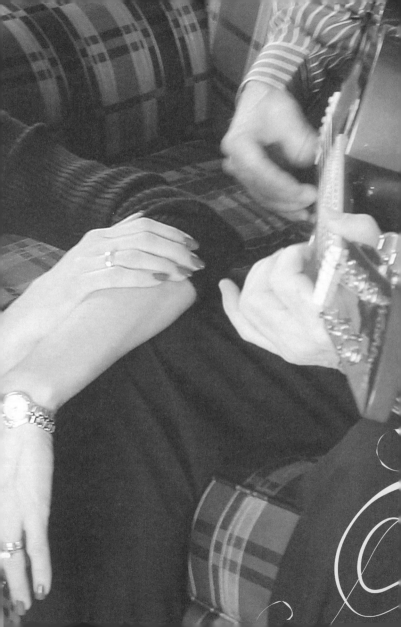

455. Say "I love you" as often as your mate needs to hear it, not just when you feel like saying it.

456. Read the Sunday paper together. Share the stories that strike you as particularly interesting, funny, or odd.

457. If you wake up first, make coffee for two.

458. For no particular reason, surprise your mate with new music by a favorite artist.

459. Do the household and yard chores together.

460. Plant your favorite flowers together in the spring.

461. Keep yourself clean and smelling fresh.

462. Grab quick, passionate kisses when it's just the two of you in an elevator.

463. Stop the elevator once in a while and share a longer kiss.

464. In the absence of elevators, quick kisses on escalators are permitted.

465. Shave your legs all the way up. He'll love it.

466. If she is sitting in a cold draft, change places with her.

467. Have a breath mint right before you get home.

468. Replace his underwear as needed.

469. Be good to each other because it is a good thing to do, not because you think you're going to get something from it.

470. Never turn down affection or make your mate work for yours.

471. Be proud to be seen together in public.

472. Give your mate many reasons to respect you. Many, many.

473. Pay attention to each other's fears and give encouragement to overcome them.

474. While at a party, surprise her by making a toast to your relationship.

475. It's better never to get drunk when you are out together, but don't be embarrassing if you do.

476. When sadness occurs, be comforting and supporting to each other.

477. When one of you is facing a difficult challenge, help carry as much of the burden as you can.

478. While at a party, let him overhear you brag about him to someone else.

479. Be sure to attend important events in each other's lives.

480. At the end of the year, be sure to acknowledge the helpful things that were done for you.

481. Always have at least one New Year's resolution about improving your relationship. Live up to it.

482. Sometimes a cliché is all that comes to mind. Don't frown when he uses one.

483. Be careful never to take out your frustrations on each other.

484. You will have a fight. Agree on the rules of engagement before you have one. Stick to the rules when you have one. Make sure "kiss and make up" is a rule.

485. Sometimes all she wants to do is talk. Listen—and don't set a time limit.

486. Learn to count to three before you get angry. Twenty-five would be even better.

487. Never make threatening statements like, "This is your last chance!" to each other.

488. When you have had a fight, be the first to make peace. It won't kill you.

489. Give each other butterfly kisses sometimes, especially when one of you is waking up.

490. Put chocolate kisses on your pillows on special occasions.

491. A quiet moment is a good time to say, "I love you."

492. Never go to sleep while you are angry with each other.

493. Understand that intimacy is a gift, not an obligation.

494. Whenever the other person makes a suggestion, give it serious consideration.

495. Ask each other questions before jumping to wrong conclusions.

496. Be willing to grovel when you are wrong. Maybe even when you aren't.

497. Understand that he wants to make you happy. Let him know when you are.

498. Learn how to distinguish between big issues and things that don't matter. Overlook those that don't matter.

499. If you are unsure of whether you can resist temptation, stay away from what may tempt you.

500. Show each other a love sign every day. When you have shown all that you can think of, start over and show them all again.

Gift Guide

Gift giving is an important component of a loving relationship—it clearly implies, "I thought of you today." Yet, as important as gift giving is, it is easy to fall into a pattern of giving the same kind of gift over and over again, eventually diluting the "you are special to me" message the gift is supposed to convey. Make sure your message isn't lost. Use these wallet guides as a helpful prompt when shopping for a unique gift that without question says, "I love you."

_ Stainless steel grooming set
_ Espresso machine
_ Messenger bag
_ iPod accessories
_ Cigar sampler
_ Leather Dopp kit
_ Vintage concert poster
_ Collector's edition of his favorite book
_ Poker chip and card set
_ Universal remote control
_ Turkey fryer
_ Hot sauce sampler
_ Digital meat thermometer
_ Personalized letter opener
_ Cologne
_ Favorite actor movie collection
_ Massage appointment
_ Dinner at his favorite restaurant

_ Monogrammed bathrobe
_ Stainless steel travel mug
_ Subscription to his favorite magazine
_ A bottle of single malt scotch
_ Crystal old-fashioned bar glasses
_ Mont Blanc pen
_ Favorite college team paraphernalia
_ Personalized business card case
_ Coffee of the month club membership
_ Tailor-made dress shirt
_ Single cup coffeemaker for his desk
_ Leather briefcase
_ Leather driving gloves
_ Noise canceling headphones
_ Swiss Army knife

_ Digital photo album
_ Backyard hammock
_ Grilling accessories
_ First Aid kit for his car
_ Aviator sunglasses
_ Favorite team baseball cap
_ Digital camera
_ Golf shirt
_ Golf balls
_ Lined moccasins
_ Rapid beverage chiller
_ Team flag
_ Leather wallet
_ Hiking poles
_ Sports binoculars
_ World travel guide
_ Mini camcorder
_ Rugged field watch
_ Water sandals
_ Electric corkscrew

PLAY FOOTSIE UNDER
THE TABLE

GREGORY E. LANG

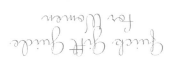

Quick Gift Guide
for Women

_ Subscription to her favorite magazine
_ New equipment for her favorite sport
_ Favorite team sweatshirt
_ Single cup coffeemaker for her desk
_ Lined gloves
_ Winter scarf
_ Portrait session
_ Chick-flick DVDs and popcorn
_ Monthly car wash for a year
_ Personal GPS device
_ Luxurious bath towels
_ A love letter
_ Manicure-pedicure appointment
_ Tea steeper and teas
_ Matching coffee mugs

_ Monogrammed bathrobe
_ Kindle
_ Bedroom slippers
_ Designer purse
_ Leather wallet
_ Compact umbrella
_ Crystal champagne stems
_ Chilled champagne
_ Crystal flower vase
_ Bath salts and scrubs
_ Scented candles
_ Bedtime reading lamp
_ Favorite author book collection
_ Wine of the month club
_ Day of spa pampering
_ iPhone
_ Perfume
_ Key chain flashlight
_ Digital camera

_ Diamond earrings
_ Antique ring
_ Heart on a chain
_ Designer sunglasses
_ Roadside emergency kit
_ One of a kind martini glasses
_ Dinner at her favorite restaurant
_ Riedel wine glasses
_ Cashmere sweater
_ Teeth whitening appointment
_ Concert tickets
_ Weekend at the beach
_ Weekend in the mountains
_ Chocolate
_ Personalized stationary
_ Digital photo album
_ Luggage
_ Breakfast in bed
_ Lotion collection

Acknowledgments

I owe a heartfelt thanks to Ron Pitkin, and the staff at Cumberland House who initially developed this book, and now also to all the great people at Sourcebooks who have taken the original idea and kicked it up a notch, making it better than ever. I hope folks will enjoy reading this book as much as I did watching it come to life.

I must thank my wonderful wife, Jill, for her reviews of the many drafts of this book, her constant support and loving attention, and for sharing her daughter, Linley, with me. I love you both. Finally, I thank my own beloved child, Meagan Katherine, who continues to be the reason I try to do no wrong, for helping me to "keep it real." I love you too, Meagan, more and more each day.

To Contact the Author
write in care of the publisher:
Sourcebooks, Inc.
P.O. Box 4410
Naperville, IL 60567-4410

or email:
gregoryelang@gmail
www.gregoryelang. com